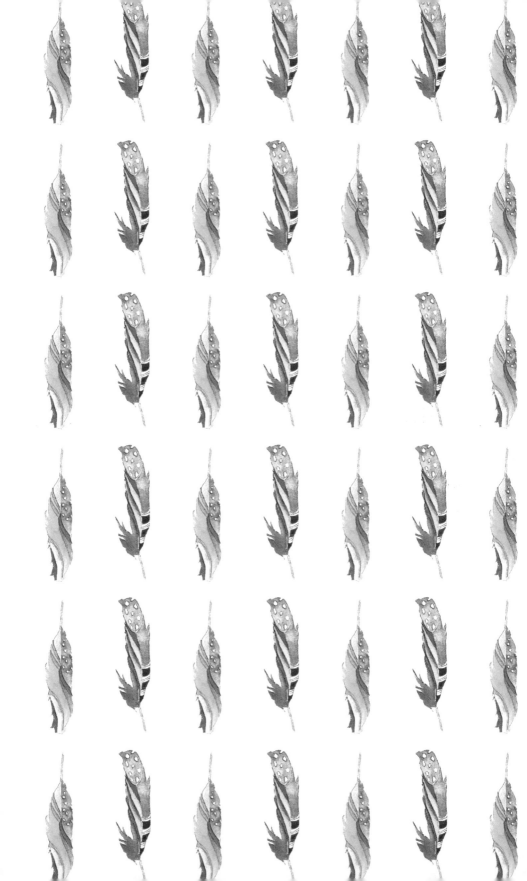

For Jake, who showed us what we were missing.
–Corky

For that little red bird that lets me know you are near.
–Natalie

Published by Orange Hat Publishing 2018

ISBN 978-1-948365-59-8 Hardcover
ISBN 978-1-948365-58-1 Paperback
Library of Congress Control Number: 2018954634

Ken the Keeper
Written by courtney kotloski
Illustrated by natalie sorrentino

www.orangehatpublishing.com

Ken the Keeper

Xo

Xo

The Gnat & Corky Series

Written by Courtney Kotloski

Illustrated by Natalie Sorrentino

"Until one has loved an animal,
a part of one's soul remains
unawakened." - Anatole France

A broken wing, a tail that won't wag,
and a story behind their eyes.

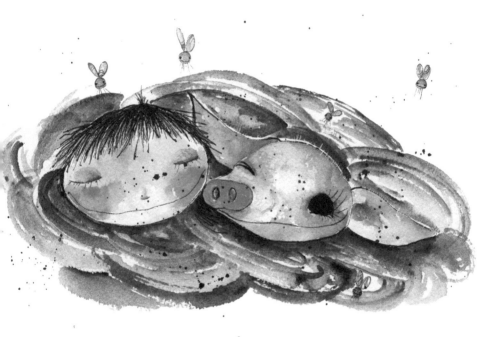

I'm the keeper of the animals,
all things great and small.

Furry, four-legged, fins, feathers;
they come to me
seeking happiness.

We speak with no words
and talk about their travels.

This one lost its way.
That one was given up, and
something led them to my
Happy Animals Club.

A stitch here.

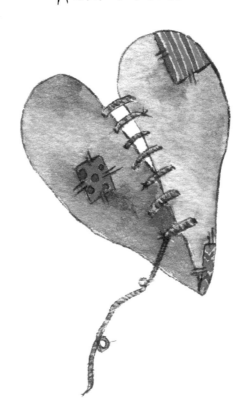

A blanket to stay warm.

A day in my hands and
their hearts begin to heal.

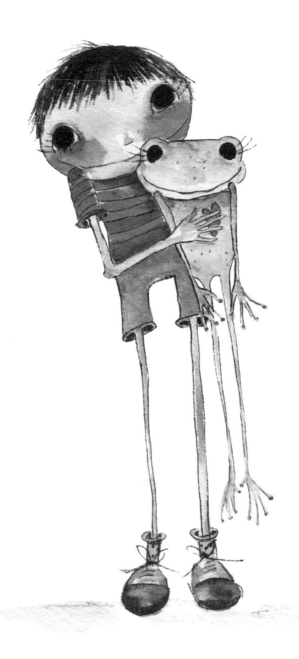

Every animal is a gift.

The bird a symbol
of grace and
honor.

The dog a champion of friendship and loyalty.

Each

creature

shows us

something

that we can

treasure in

each other.

I am the keeper, mending, caring for, and loving all animals until they are ready to be set free.

Slither.

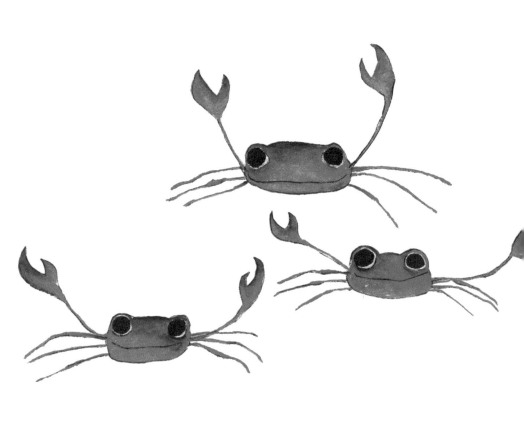

Crawl.

Slide.

Swim.

Scurry.

Run.

Jump.

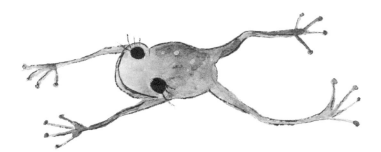

Hop.

Fly.

Soar.

Meet Ken the Keeper

At nine years old, Ken started Happy Animals Club.
His mission is to rescue animals, give them the
highest standard of care, and find good homes for
them. Happy Animals Club is a no-kill shelter in
the Davao region of the Philippines. The shelter
is funded by the generosity of people all over the
world. You can visit www.happyanimalsclub.org to
learn more and make a donation to help the animals
in Ken's care. Be a Keeper!

Hey!
Did you know Gnat & Corky have
a collection of books?
Visit www.gnatandcorky.com to find
more titles and collect them all. You can
also answer Gnat & Corky's questions
and have a chance to be the next book!